About this book

You don't have to be a master chef to roast a chicken or make a chocolate mousse, but you do need to understand a few cooking terms and techniques.

Each recipe in this book explains either a basic method of cooking, such as broiling, frying, baking and roasting, or a cooking term, such as working in, beating, creaming, whisking, folding and kneading.

Once you know how to fry a slice of bread, you will be able to fry sausages or bacon, too—the food may change, but the basic method remains the same.

The same is true of cooking terms—once you know how to beat a mixture, you can make pancakes, fruit popovers, banana cake or an apple and almond cake —the ingredients change, the technique doesn't.

After you have made some of the recipes in this book, you will know why certain foods should be cooked in certain ways, as well as how to prepare them. Try experimenting and create your own original recipes.

First published in the United States of America 1982 by Philomel Books, a division of the Putnam Publishing Group, 200 Madison Avenue, New York, N.Y. 10016. First published in Great Britain 1982 by Methuen Children's Books, Ltd., in association with Walker Books, Ltd., London. Printed in Italy.

Library of Congress Cataloging in Publication Data
John, Sue.
The how-to cookbook.
Summary: Suggested recipes introduce basic cooking techniques and terms.
1. Cookery—Juvenile literature. [1. Cookery]
I. Hardcastle, Nick, ill. II. Bull, Carolyn, ill.
III. Escreet, Judith, ill. IV. Title.
TX652.5.J55 1982 641.5′123 82-3642
ISBN 0-399-20890-9 AACR2

Contents

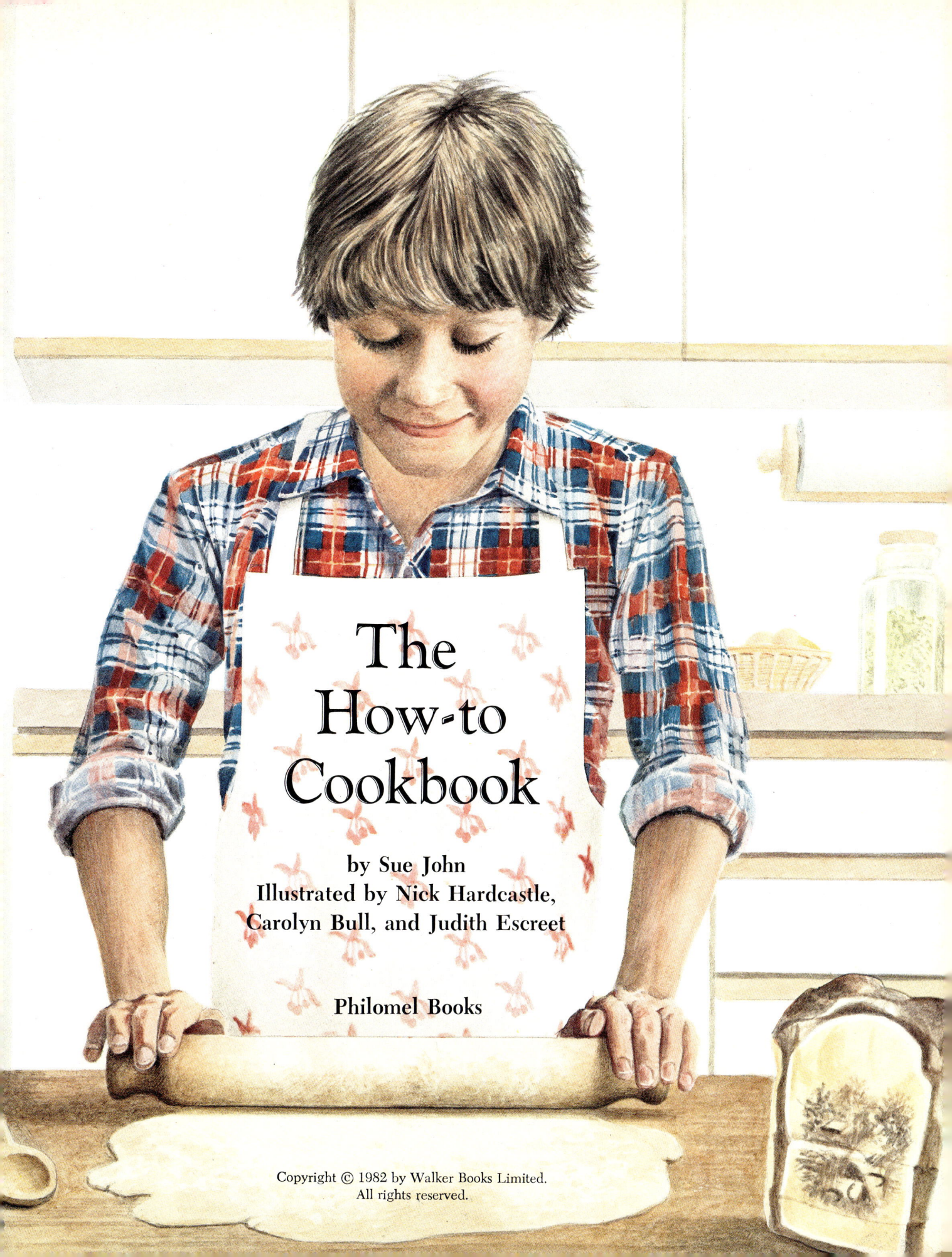

The How-to Cookbook

by Sue John
Illustrated by Nick Hardcastle,
Carolyn Bull, and Judith Escreet

Philomel Books

grater

measuring cup

How to use this book

This means that there is an alternative way to make a recipe.

Before you start:
- Wear an apron so that your clothes won't get splashed or stained.
- Read a recipe from start to finish to be sure you have everything you need before you begin.
- Wash your hands before handling food.
- Put all the necessary ingredients on your work surface. If you will be using butter or margarine, be sure that it is soft for spreading.
- Assemble all the cooking equipment you need so that you don't have to stop in the middle of a recipe to find something.
- Use a kitchen timer, if you have one, to ensure proper cooking times.

While you cook:
- Always use pot holders or oven mitts when handling hot pots or pans.
- Pick up a knife by its handle, not by its blade.
- Keep your work surface as neat as possible, so that you can see what you are doing.
- If anything spills on the floor, mop it up immediately to avoid accidents.

After you finish:
- Put away any unused ingredients.
- Wash, dry and put away all your equipment.
- Clean your work surface.

Helpful Hints:
- When beating or creaming ingredients in a bowl, rest the bowl on a damp cloth to prevent it from slipping.
- When using a rolling pin, sprinkle flour on it as well as on your work surface to keep the food from sticking.

- When rolling out dough, rest your fingers lightly on the rolling pin and gently roll it forward and backward, not from side to side.
- The easiest way to wash fruits and vegetables is to put them in a colander and run cold water over them.
- When using apples or bananas, don't cut them before you need them, or they will discolor.
- Before taking hot pans or dishes out of the oven, be sure to have a hot plate or trivet nearby to put them on.
- Keep the handles of any pots and pans cooking on the stove turned inward, so that you can't knock them over accidentally.
- Serve hot foods immediately, using plates that you have warmed in a very slow oven.

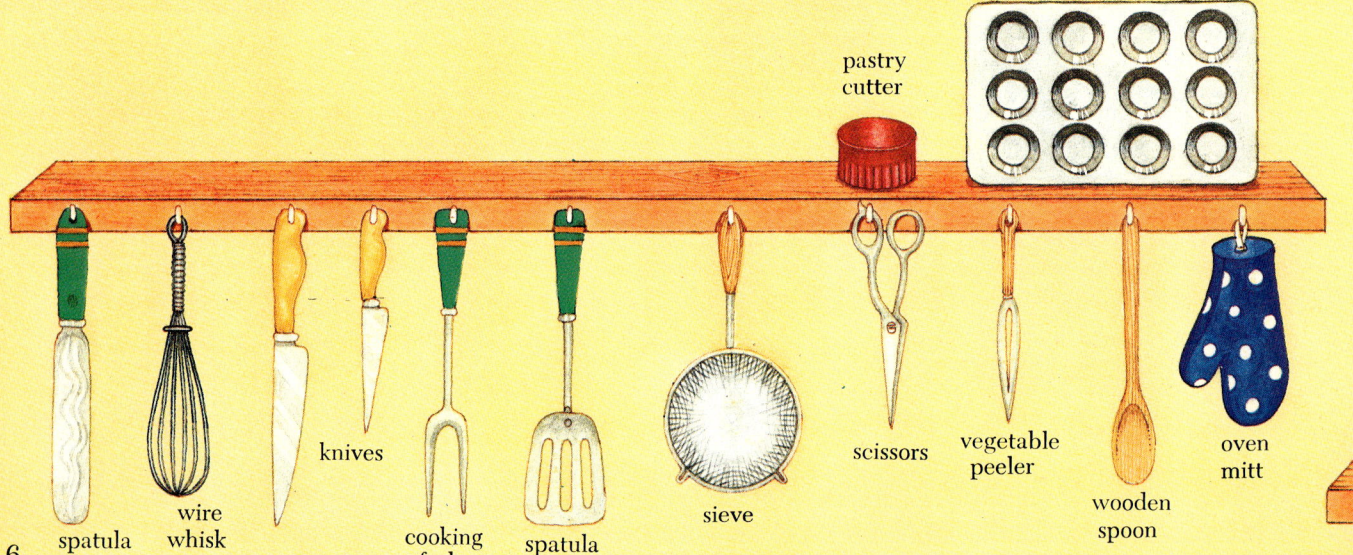
muffin tin

pastry cutter

spatula

wire whisk

knives

cooking fork

spatula

sieve

scissors

vegetable peeler

wooden spoon

oven mitt

bowls   colander   wire rack   loaf pan

How to measure

The system of measurement used in the United States is different from the metric system most countries use. In the U.S. the liquid measure of one cup is used to measure both liquid and dry ingredients. The metric system measures dry ingredients by weight (grams and kilograms) and liquids by milliliters and liters. Grams are abbreviated g and liters are abbreviated l.

Liquid measure

U.S.	Metric
1 oz. (ounce)	about 30 milliliters
½ cup	about 120 milliliters
1 cup (½ pint)	about ¼ liter
1 quart	about 1 liter

Dry measure

U.S.	Metric
1 oz. (ounce)	about 28 grams
1 pound	about 450 grams

Dry ingredients can be measured in tablespoons, too. One heaping tablespoon of flour amounts to 25 grams of flour.

How to use the stove and oven

Be careful whenever you use the stove or oven. Always use pot holders or oven mitts when handling hot pots and pans. Be sure to turn oven and stove dials to "off" when you have finished cooking.

Each recipe will tell you the correct temperature at which to set your oven. Be sure to preheat the oven to the temperature called for in the recipe before putting food in to bake. Allow 15 or 20 minutes for the oven to preheat. Fahrenheit is abbreviated F.

Equipment

This is a list of all the cooking equipment you will need for the recipes in this book. Always ask an adult or older friend for help if you aren't sure how to use something.

A few explanations:

Chopping board: always use this when cutting, chopping, or slicing ingredients.

Grater: used to break food into small pieces. Watch your knuckles when you use a grater!

Spatula: a flexible knife that is very useful for spreading icing, scraping bowls and lifting cookies.

bowls:
  large
  shallow
  small
breadboard
broiling pan
cake pan
can opener
chopping board
colander
cookie sheet
cooking fork
dishcloth
dish towel
forks
frying pan (small)
grater
knives:
  large, sharp
  small, sharp
  table
loaf pan
measuring cups

measuring spoons
muffin tins
oven mitts
oven-proof dishes
paper towels
pastry cutters
Pyrex mixing bowl
roasting pan
rolling pin
saucepan
scissors
serving dishes, plates
  and bowls
sieve
spatula
spoons:
  table
  tea
  wooden
tongs
vegetable peeler
wire whisk

cake pan

Basic cooking methods

Broiling, frying, baking and roasting are four basic methods of cooking. Different foods adapt to different methods.

Broiling is an easy way to cook because the food doesn't need much preparation. It's also quick, because food is placed close to the heat.

Food that you want to broil should be thin, so that the inside can cook thoroughly, without the outside burning. Meats should be lean—fatty foods spit and burn. Lean bacon, hamburgers, steak, fish fillets, chicken pieces, thin chops and bread are all ideal foods for broiling.

Some foods must be broiled on both sides. Use a spatula, tongs or cooking fork to turn over foods.

Some foods, such as bread (see p. 11), are broiled plain, or have their own fats, such as bacon. Other foods, such as sole fillets (see p. 10), need a little oil or butter added to them to keep them from drying out.

Turn the broiler on high and put the food into the broiling pan. Remember to keep thicker foods, such as chicken pieces, farther from the heat so that they can cook more gradually. Watch the food constantly to be sure that it doesn't burn. Turn down the heat if necessary.

Frying is another quick way to cook. You can fry bacon, mushrooms, eggs, tomatoes, potatoes, pancakes, fish, hamburgers and sandwiches. Bread is easy to fry (see Fried melting slices, p. 12), and so are fruit slices (see p. 13).

Use a spatula to lift foods in and out of a frying pan, and a spatula, tongs or cooking fork to turn foods over while they cook.

Fry food in a layer of melted butter or oil. You may have to add more oil or butter while you fry. Be sure that you turn the handle of the pan inward so that you can't knock it over accidentally.

Baking is also a simple way to cook—the food usually doesn't need any further attention once it's in the oven. You can bake casseroles of vegetables or meat or noodles, as well as many desserts such as cakes, pastries, pies, muffins and fruit (see Vanilla apricots, pp. 14–15).

Roasting foods in the oven is a classic and easy way to cook. You can roast cuts of beef, veal, pork and lamb, as well as chicken (see Chicken with rosemary, pp. 16–17), turkey, duck and vegetables (see Roast zucchini, pp. 16–17).

The food cooks in an open pan. Fat comes out of most foods as they cook, but you need to add butter to roast chicken, veal or turkey. Spoon the fat or butter back over your food from time to time while it cooks to keep it from drying out. This is called basting. Roast meat in a 425° F. oven for 20 minutes and then lower the heat to 375° F. for the remaining cooking time, so that your food is tender inside and crisp outside.

It's economical to bake or roast two dishes at the same time. The hottest part of most ovens is toward the top. You can adjust the height of the shelves before turning on the heat. Turn on the oven to the higher temperature that you need, and bake a second dish on a lower shelf if it needs a lower cooking temperature. Keep a 2-cm space between dishes on the same shelf, so that the heat can flow around them evenly.

Bubbling cheese and fish

Fish fillets are ideal for broiling. This tasty recipe is for 1 person, but you could fit three or four fish fillets on a broiling pan if you wished to expand the recipe to feed more people. Always use oven mitts when putting foods into or taking them out of the oven. Preheat the broiler.

Ingredients

1 fillet of sole
1 tomato
salt and pepper
about 20 g butter or margarine
1 or 2 thin slices cheddar or
　　Swiss cheese

1. Wipe the fish with a piece of damp paper towel. Using a small, sharp knife, cut the tomato in half.

2. Put the fish, skin-side down, on the broiling pan. Put the tomato halves, cut-sides up, beside the fish. Sprinkle a little salt and pepper over everything.

3. Using a small, sharp knife, cut the butter into small pieces. Scatter the pieces on top of the fish and the tomatoes.

4. Put the broiling pan under the hot broiler for 4 or 5 minutes. Carefully remove the pan from the heat and put the cheese on top of the fish.

5. Put the pan back under the heat and broil the food for another 1 or 2 minutes, until the cheese melts and turns a golden brown. Remove the pan from the heat.

6. Using a spatula, carefully lift the fish and the tomato halves onto a warm plate.

☞ Tomatoes broiled with bacon are also delicious. Put the tomato halves and bacon slices under the hot broiler. After about 2 minutes, use a cooking fork to turn over the bacon. Broil the other side for 2 minutes.

Toasted nuts and bananas

This recipe makes a delicious snack for 1 person. Like most of the broiling recipes, it is quick and easy to prepare. Preheat the broiler.

Ingredients

1 slice whole wheat or other brown bread
butter or margarine
peanut butter
1 medium-sized banana

1. Put the bread on the broiling pan. Using oven mitts, put the pan under the hot broiler and toast the bread on one side.

2. Remove the pan from the heat. Put the toast on a chopping board. Use a table knife to spread butter generously over the untoasted side.

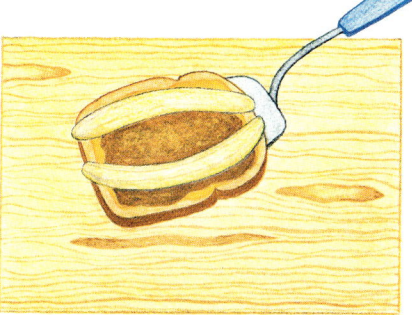

3. Use the table knife to spread peanut butter generously on top of the butter.

4. Peel the banana and throw away the skin. Use a small, sharp knife to cut the banana in half lengthwise.

5. Put the two banana halves on top of the peanut butter. Use a spatula to lift the bread back onto the broiling pan.

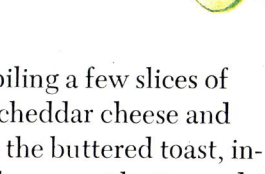

6. Put the pan under the hot broiler and broil for 1 or 2 minutes until the banana begins to turn brown.

7. Remove the pan from the heat. Use the spatula to lift the bread onto a warm plate.

☞ Try broiling a few slices of Colby or cheddar cheese and apples on the buttered toast, instead of the peanut butter and bananas.

Fried melting slices

This easy-to-prepare recipe makes a good snack for 1 person. Use brown or white bread, sliced thinly so that it will fry thoroughly and quickly. Try broiling or frying bacon or sausages to eat with the fried bread.

Ingredients

1 medium-sized egg
2 tablespoons milk
pinch of salt
25 g butter
2 thin slices bread

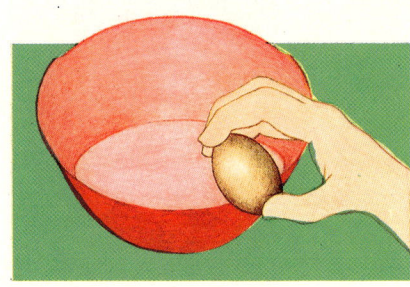

1. Hold the ends of the egg between your thumb and index finger. Gently but firmly, tap the middle of the egg on the edge of a shallow bowl.

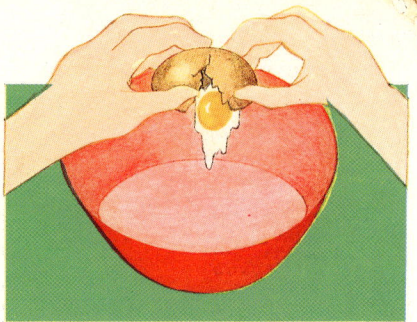

2. Using both hands, pull apart the two halves of the egg shell. Let the egg drop into the bowl below it.

3. Use a fork or a wire whisk to beat the egg (see p. 19 and pp. 26–27) so that the yolk and white mix together thoroughly.

4. Add the milk and salt to the bowl. Use the fork or wire whisk to beat the mixture thoroughly.

5. Put the butter into a small frying pan. Melt it over medium heat until the butter begins to froth. If your pan is large, add a little more butter.

6. Use your fingers to put one slice of bread into the egg mixture. Use a spatula to lift up the bread so that any extra egg drips back into the bowl.

7. Carefully slide the bread into the melted butter in the pan. Repeat steps 6 and 7 with the other slice of bread.

8. Fry for about 1 minute on each side until the bread turns a light, golden brown. This is delicious served plain or with maple syrup or a sprinkling of cinnamon.

Golden brown apples

This recipe makes a delicious dessert for 1 person when it is served with heavy cream or vanilla ice cream. Don't peel the apples until just before you are ready to fry them, or they will discolor.

Ingredients
1 large, crisp eating apple
25 g butter
1 level tablespoon soft brown sugar
½ teaspoon powdered cinnamon

1. Using a small, sharp knife, cut the apple into quarters. Cut out the core and use the knife to remove a thin outer layer of the skin from each quarter.

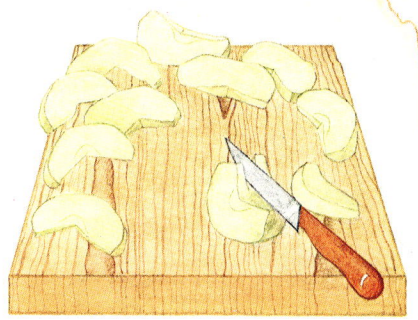

2. Cut each peeled quarter into thin slices. You will get about three slices from each quarter.

3. Melt the butter in a small frying pan over low heat.

4. Using a spatula, lift the apple slices and carefully put them into the pan.

5. Cook for 1 or 2 minutes, gently shaking the pan from time to time to keep the apples from sticking. Add a little more butter if needed.

6. Sprinkle the sugar and cinnamon over the apples. Turn the heat down and over a low flame cook for 1 more minute, until the sugar melts and coats the apple slices.

7. Using the spatula, lift the apple slices into a warm dessert bowl or plate. Pour any juices left in the pan over the slices.

☞ If you peel off the skins from bananas and cut them in half lengthwise, you can fry them too. Well-drained, canned pineapple rings are also delicious when fried.

Baked potato slices

Like most baked dishes, this recipe for 4 people needs no further attention once it is in the oven. Serve this with rosemary chicken (see pp. 16–17) and a salad for a delicious meal. Preheat the oven to 375° F.

Ingredients
4 medium-sized potatoes
50 g butter or margarine
100 g cheddar cheese
salt and pepper
150 ml milk

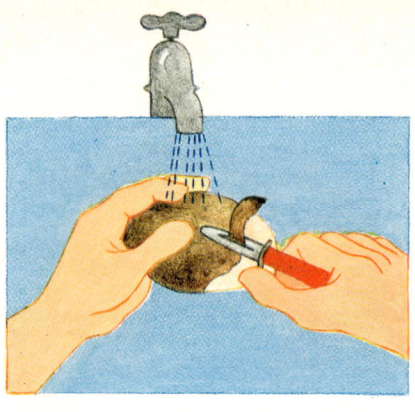

1. Using a vegetable peeler, peel the skin from the potatoes. Rinse the potatoes under cold, running water from time to time while you are peeling them.

2. Using a small, sharp knife, cut the potatoes into thin slices. Put the slices into a large bowl of cold water.

6. Put a layer of potato slices in the dish. Sprinkle some grated cheese and a little salt and pepper over the slices.

7. Keep alternating layers of potato slices and grated cheese until you use them up, ending with a layer of potatoes on top.

8. Pour the milk over the potatoes and cheese.

Vanilla apricots

Fruits baked whole have a wonderful flavor and keep their shapes. This is a delicious dessert served hot or cold. Preheat the oven to 350° F.

Ingredients
12 fresh apricots
4–5 tablespoons sugar
vanilla extract

1. Arrange the apricots in a shallow, oven-proof dish. They should fit snugly.

2. Pour cold water into the dish to a depth of 2 cm.

3. Hold a small piece of the butter in a piece of paper towel. Rub it all around the inside of a shallow, one-liter, oven-proof dish to grease it.

4. Transfer the potatoes to a colander in the sink to drain off the water.

5. Using a coarse grater, grate the cheese.

9. Using a small, sharp knife, cut the remaining butter into small pieces. Scatter them on top of the potatoes.

10. Bake in the preheated oven for 1¼ hours, until the top layer of potatoes is crisp and golden.

☞ An onion chopped into small pieces and sprinkled over each layer of potatoes and cheese is a tasty addition to this recipe. You might also try placing a sprig of fresh thyme or other herb over each layer.

3. Sprinkle the sugar over the fruit. Add a few drops of vanilla extract to the water around the apricots.

4. Bake in the preheated oven for about 1 hour. Carefully remove the dish from the oven.

☞ Try baking plums or small peaches in the same way. If you use large peaches, cut them in half first, remove the pits, and put them into the dish cut-sides down.

Chicken with rosemary

Be sure that the giblets have been removed before you put the chicken in to roast. If you use one that was frozen, it must be completely defrosted before roasting. Preheat the oven to 425° F.

Ingredients

1 medium-sized roasting chicken
50 g soft butter
1 sprig fresh, or 1 level teaspoon dried, rosemary
salt and pepper
½ lemon

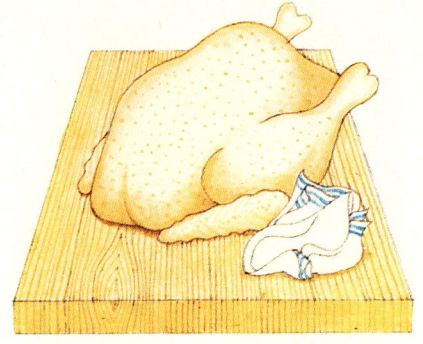

1. Using a piece of damp paper towel, wipe the chicken inside and out. Put the chicken onto a chopping board.

2. Put the butter on a small plate. Using scissors, snip rosemary leaves over the butter. Season with a little salt and pepper.

6. Put chicken in the oven and roast for 20 minutes. Carefully remove the pan and, using a tablespoon, spoon melted butter back over the chicken. This process is called basting.

7. Put the pan back into the oven and lower the heat to 375° F. Cook another 40 minutes, basting the chicken once or twice during this time.

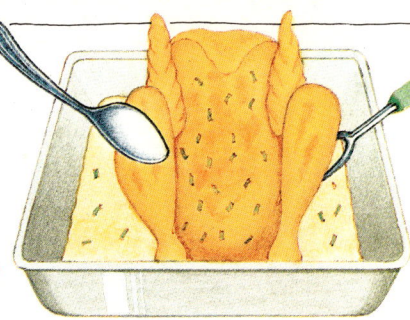

8. Carefully remove the pan from the oven. Using a cooking fork and a large spoon to hold the sides of the chicken, turn it over so that the breast is facing up.

Roast zucchini

This recipe for 4 people makes a delicious accompaniment to the Chicken with rosemary. Once you have completed steps 1–3, simply put the pan with the zucchini in the 375° F. oven for the last 40 minutes of the chicken's cooking time.

Ingredients

4 medium-sized zucchini
25 g butter
4 tablespoons vegetable oil
salt

1. Using a small, sharp knife, cut off the ends of the zucchini and throw them away. Cut the zucchini into slices 1.5 cm thick.

2. Add the butter and oil to a small roasting pan. Put the pan into a 375° F. oven for 5 minutes.

3. Using the flat blade of a table knife, mix everything together.

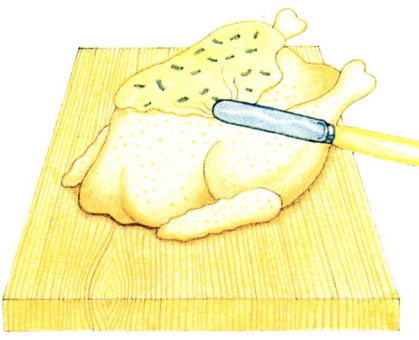

4. Using the table knife, spread half the butter over the breast of the chicken.

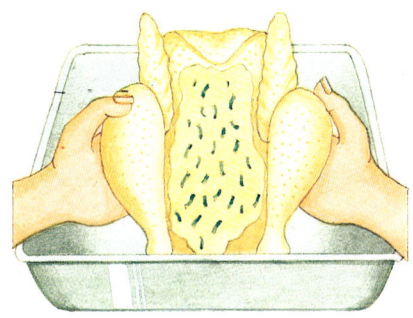

5. Put the chicken into a roasting pan, breast down. Use the knife to spread the rest of the butter over the chicken.

9. Squeeze the juice from the lemon over the chicken.

10. Put the pan back into the oven for another 20–30 minutes, so that the chicken finishes cooking and the skin on the breast turns brown.

11. Carefully lift the pan from the oven. Using the cooking fork and spoon, lift the chicken onto a warm serving plate and pour the juices over it.

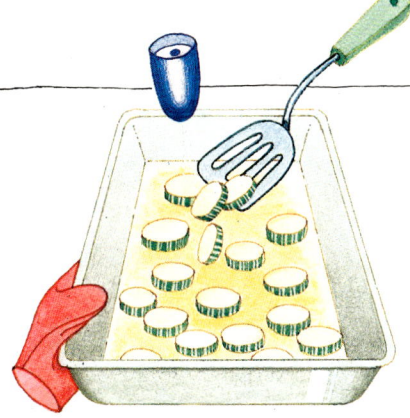

3. Remove the pan from the oven. Using a spatula, carefully put the zucchini into the butter and oil. Season them with a little salt.

4. Put the pan back into the oven and roast for about 40 minutes. Baste the zucchini twice while they cook (see step 6 of Chicken with rosemary).

5. Remove the pan from the oven. Using a spatula, lift the zucchini into a serving dish or arrange them around the roasted chicken.

Basic cooking terms

Once you understand the basic cooking terms, you will be able to prepare almost any dish that you like.

Working in is a way to mix together flour and fat, such as butter or margarine. If you need to add other ingredients, such as sugar, do so after you work in the fat.

Working in is always done by hand and, usually, in a large bowl. It's a "dry" way to mix. To keep the mixture dry, the ingredients must be cold. Store the fat in the refrigerator until just before you use it, rinse your hands in cold water before working in ingredients and, if possible, work on a cold surface.

Working in is often the first stage of a recipe, as in Lemon tarts (see pp. 20–21). Different flours and fats may be used in various recipes, but the technique is always the same. Important words to remember are: lightly, quickly and cool.

Beating is one way to mix together various ingredients, as in Batter (see p. 22). If you don't have an electric beater, you'll need lots of physical energy for good results. The harder you beat, the more evenly blended, smoother and lighter your mixture will be.

Beating is usually done with a fork or a wooden spoon. Put your mixing bowl on a damp cloth to keep it from slipping. Don't be afraid to beat the mixture hard, and keep going!

Creaming is a way to mix together sugar and fat, such as butter or margarine (see pp. 24–25). You must work quite hard, so that air gets into the mixture. This will give a lighter, more evenly mixed product.

Use a wooden spoon to press ingredients together against the base and sides of a mixing bowl. Put the bowl on a damp cloth to keep it from slipping. Use a spatula to scrape the mixture from the bowl and the spoon from time to time.

Finely ground sugar is good for creaming. The fat must be soft before you use it, so keep it at room temperature beforehand. Soft margarine is ideal to use.

Your final result should be light, soft and, of course, creamy.

Whisking means to work as much air as possible into ingredients, as in Chocolate mousse (see pp. 26–27). Whether you use a wire whisk, an egg beater or an electric beater, you must work with a large, spotlessly clean and dry mixing bowl. The recipe may call for an ingredient to be whisked on its own or together with a few ingredients. Air is the only ingredient that makes the mixture light, so it is important to whisk thoroughly.

Kneading is always done by hand to a dough mixture. For easier handling, knead on a work surface that you have sprinkled with flour.

   The dough may require gentle or strong kneading. Knead a pastry or cookie dough (see pp. 20–21 and pp. 28–29) by pressing it gently with your fingertips. Turn the dough around, folding the outside edges into the center as you knead. Continue turning and folding until the dough is smooth.

Folding is a way of mixing gently, without stirring. To fold, you simply lift the ingredients from the bottom to the top and then fold them over.

Shortcrust pastry

Shortcrust pastry is the easiest kind to make. Once you know how to make it, you can bake pies and tarts. The flour can be white or whole-wheat. Keep the margarine in the refrigerator until you need it.

Ingredients
150 g flour
pinch of salt
75 g margarine

1. Sift the flour and salt into a large mixing bowl.

2. Cut the margarine into small pieces and drop them into the mixing bowl.

Lemon tarts

You can use shortcrust pastry to make these delicious pastry shells. For a tasty treat, fill them with lemon curd or lemon curd marmalade, available at your supermarket or gourmet food shop. Or, after baking the shells, you can substitute any of the fruit fillings on p. 21. Preheat the oven to 425° F.

Ingredients
shortcrust pastry
about 6 tablespoons lemon curd
  or lemon curd marmalade
confectioner's sugar

1. Sprinkle some flour over your work surface and place the dough on it.

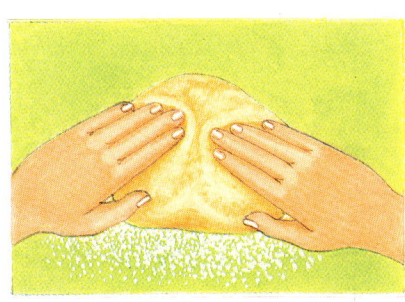

2. Gently knead (see p. 19) the dough for about 1 minute. Roll it into a ball.

6. Using the spatula, lift each circle and gently place it over a hollow in the muffin tin. Then, using your fingertips, press the dough down so that it lines each hollow.

7. Collect the scraps of pastry and repeat steps 2–6.

8. Using a teaspoon and your little finger, put one spoonful of lemon curd into each of the pastry shells.

3. Using only your fingertips, lift some of the mixture about 10 cm above the bowl. Quickly and gently rub it between your fingertips, letting it fall back down into the bowl.

4. Lift and rub until the mixture looks like fresh breadcrumbs or dry sand.

5. Using a spatula, stir in two tablespoons of cold water to form a dough. Add another tablespoon of water if necessary. The pastry is now ready to roll out, fill and bake.

3. With your fingertips resting gently on a floured rolling pin, roll out the dough until it is about 1 cm thick.

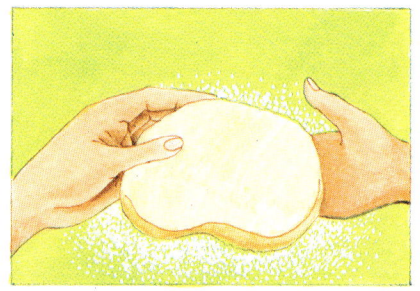

4. Slide your hands under the dough and turn it halfway around. Roll it out again until it is 0.5 cm thick.

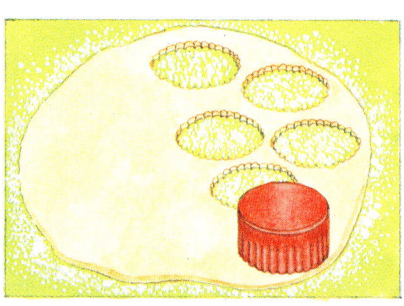

5. Using an 8 cm-diameter, fluted pastry cutter, cut out as many circles as possible from the pastry.

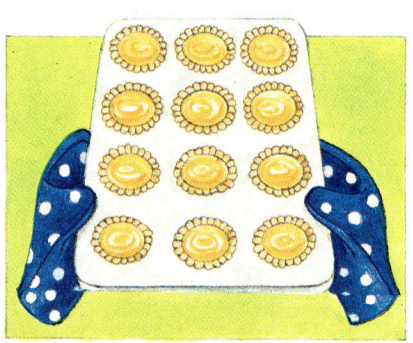

9. Bake in the preheated oven for about 15 minutes until the pastry is a light golden brown. Remove the muffin tin from the oven.

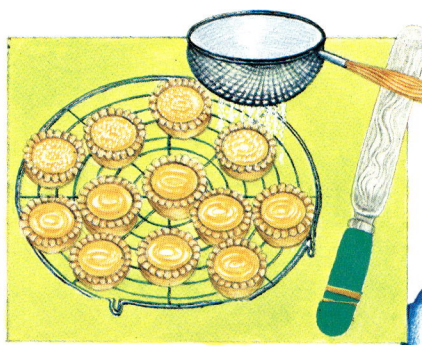

10. Using a spatula, carefully lift the tarts onto a cooling rack. Sift a little confectioner's sugar over the tops of the tarts when they have cooled.

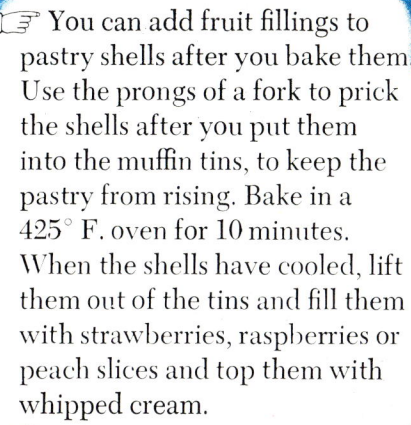

☞ You can add fruit fillings to pastry shells after you bake them. Use the prongs of a fork to prick the shells after you put them into the muffin tins, to keep the pastry from rising. Bake in a 425° F. oven for 10 minutes. When the shells have cooled, lift them out of the tins and fill them with strawberries, raspberries or peach slices and top them with whipped cream.

Batter

Be sure that you beat this batter well, until there are no lumps in it. The smoother the mixture is, the lighter the final result will be. You can use a combination of half white flour and half whole-wheat flour if you like.

Ingredients

100 g all-purpose flour
large pinch of salt
1 large egg
275 ml milk
½ teaspoon baking powder

1. Sift the flour and salt into a large mixing bowl. Use a wooden spoon to make a hole in the center of the mixture.

2. Hold the ends of the egg between your thumb and index finger. Gently but firmly, tap the middle of the egg on the edge of the bowl.

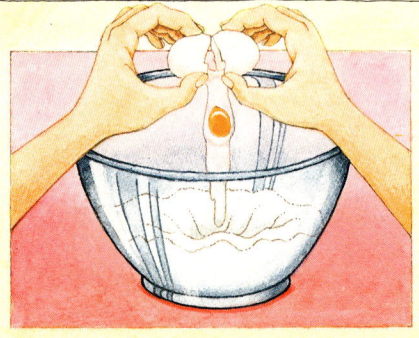

3. Using both hands, pull apart the two halves of the egg shell. Let the egg drop into the "hole" in the flour mixture below.

4. Add about half of the milk. Using a wooden spoon, beat the mixture with an over-and-over motion. Start in the center of the bowl and, gradually, mix in the flour from the edges.

5. Add the rest of the milk and beat the mixture well, until it is smooth. Now the batter is ready. Use it to make Fruit popovers (see below) or Thin pancakes (see p. 23).

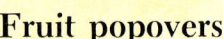

Fruit popovers

You can prepare the batter for these popovers up to two hours before you bake them, but be sure to beat it again before putting it into the muffin tins. Popovers are best fresh from the oven, so plan to enjoy these just as soon as they are baked. Preheat the oven to 425° F.

Ingredients

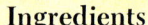

small piece of butter
batter
raisins

1. Grease the hollows of muffin tins with the butter. Put two tablespoons of the batter into each hollow. Add a few raisins to each hollow.

2. Bake in the preheated oven for about 15 minutes, until the batter puffs up. Remove the tray from the oven. Use a spatula to take out the popovers and serve immediately.

Thin pancakes

You can make delicious pancakes with the batter recipe on p. 22. As you cook, keep the pancakes warm by stacking them on a plate placed over a saucepan of very hot water. This recipe makes 10 or 12 thin pancakes.

Ingredients
batter (see p. 22)
about 30 g butter
sugar
lemon wedges

1. In a small frying pan, melt one tablespoon of butter over medium heat.

2. Put about two tablespoons of batter into the middle of the frying pan.

3. Gently tip the pan around to make the batter form a circle about 15 cm across.

4. Using a spatula, loosen the edges of the pancake. They will be a light golden brown underneath when the pancake is ready to be turned over.

5. Turn the pancake over with the spatula and cook until evenly browned. Lift the pancake onto the warm plate.

6. Repeat steps 1–5 until you use up all the batter. When ready to serve, lift the pancake onto a heated plate.

7. Roll the pancakes up and sprinkle a little sugar over each one. Serve with wedges of lemon to squeeze over the pancakes.

☞ Cut apples, bananas, pears, peaches or apricots into slices. Put a few slices on top of each pancake and add a spoonful of ice cream. The hot pancakes and cold ice cream are a tasty combination.

Banana cake

This is a delicious way to use up bananas that are too ripe. Cut the baked cake into thin slices and serve either plain or with butter. Preheat the oven to 350° F.

Ingredients

75 g soft margarine
125 g sugar
2 bananas
2 medium-sized eggs
200 g all-purpose flour
1 level teaspoon baking powder
small piece of butter

1. Put the margarine and sugar into a large mixing bowl to cream them.

2. Using a wooden spoon, work them together by pressing them very hard against the base and sides of the bowl. When the mixture is light, soft and creamy, it's ready to use.

6. Beat (see p. 18 and step 4 of Batter) everything together for 1 minute.

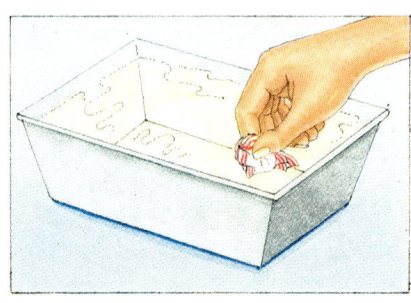

7. Holding a small piece of butter in a piece of paper towel, rub it all around the inside of a cake pan.

8. Sprinkle a tablespoon of flour into the pan and shake it around. Since the flour sticks to the butter, you will see if you missed any places and can then add butter to them.

12. Put them on a flat surface and carefully lift off the pan.

13. Turn the cake right-side up and leave it to cool.

Apple and almond cake

For another tasty and nutritious dessert or snack follow the recipe for Banana cake, but substitute apples for bananas. For a round cake, use a greased, floured, 20 cm-diameter cake pan.

Ingredients

75 g soft margarine
125 g sugar
2 eating apples
25 g slivered almonds
2 medium-sized eggs
200 g all-purpose flour
1 level teaspoon baking powder

3. Peel the bananas and throw away the skins. Use a fork to mash the bananas in a shallow bowl. Add them to the large mixing bowl.

4. Add the eggs to the mixing bowl (see steps 2 and 3 of Batter, p. 22, to break the eggs).

5. Sift the flour and baking powder into the bowl.

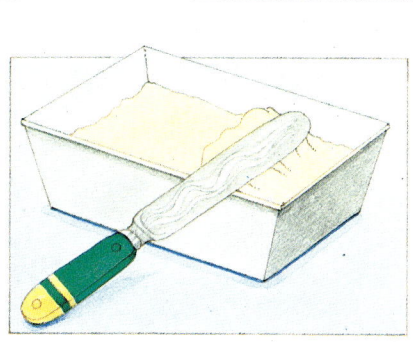

9. Scrape the mixture into the pan. Use a spatula to spread it around evenly.

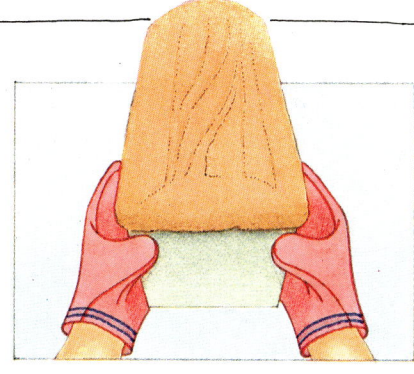

10. Bake in the center of the pre-heated oven 40–50 minutes. The cake is done when it has risen, and when it leaves the sides of the pan if you shake it gently. Take it out of the oven.

11. Let the cake sit for 5 minutes. Then put a wire rack on top of the pan and turn the rack and pan upside down.

1. Follow steps 1 and 2 of the Banana cake recipe. Peel and grate the apples. Add the apples and the almonds to the bowl. Follow steps 4–13 of the Banana cake recipe.

2. Once the baked cake has cooled, you can sift some confectioner's sugar over the top. Slice the cake and serve it plain or with butter.

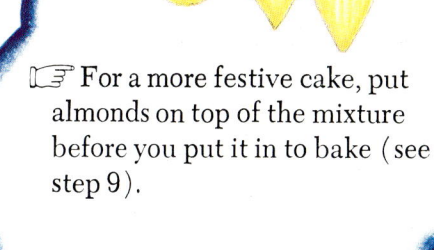

☞ For a more festive cake, put almonds on top of the mixture before you put it in to bake (see step 9).

Chocolate mousse

Whisked egg whites make this dessert for 4 people as light as air. You can use a wire whisk, an egg beater or an electric beater. Before you start, be sure that the mixing bowl is spotlessly clean and dry.

Ingredients
100 g plain baking chocolate
4 medium-sized eggs
4 tablespoons heavy cream

1. Put water into a medium-sized saucepan until it's about one-third full. Bring the water to a boil.

2. While you're waiting for the water to boil, break the chocolate into small pieces and put them into a Pyrex mixing bowl. The bowl has to be the right size to rest on the rim of the saucepan.

6. Tip the yolk back and forth from one half of the shell to the other, letting the egg white drop into the bowl below.

7. Tip the yolk into the bowl of melted chocolate. Repeat steps 4–7 with the other eggs.

8. Pour the cream into the melted chocolate and yolk mixture. Stir with a large spoon.

Hot peach surprise

When you whisk egg whites and fold in sugar, you make meringue —delicious topping for many desserts that are baked in the oven. Preheat the oven to 400° F.

Ingredients
4 ripe peaches or 1 large can of
    halved peaches
powdered cinnamon
2 medium-sized eggs
100 g sugar

1. If you are using fresh peaches, cut them in half with a small, sharp knife and throw away the pits.

2. Put the peaches, cut-sides up, into a shallow, oven-proof dish. Use a teaspoon to sprinkle a little cinnamon over each peach half.

3. When the water boils, turn off the heat. Carefully put the mixing bowl on top of the saucepan. Leave it there until the chocolate melts.

4. While you are waiting, separate the eggs. Hold the ends of one egg between your thumb and index finger. Gently but firmly, tap the middle of it on the edge of a clean mixing bowl.

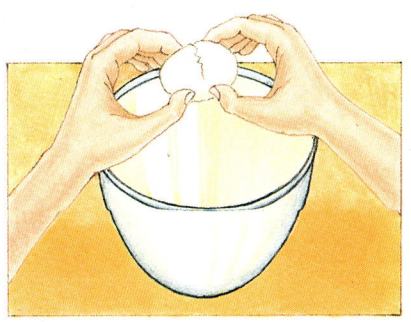

5. Using both hands, carefully pull apart the two halves of the egg shell, holding them over the bowl.

9. Using a wire whisk, whisk the egg whites briskly until they are very fluffy and firm. The mixture should stand up in peaks when you lift the whisk.

10. Using a metal tablespoon, gently fold the egg whites into the chocolate. Do not stir—simply lift the chocolate from bottom to top and fold through the egg whites.

11. Holding the bowl at an angle, quickly spoon the mixture into four individual dishes. Put them in the refrigerator for 1 hour, to set.

3. Separate the eggs (see steps 4–6 above). Put the yolks into a bowl, cover and keep in the refrigerator for up to two days. Whisk the whites (see step 9, above).

4. Using a metal tablespoon, fold the sugar into the egg whites. Do not stir—simply lift the egg whites from bottom to top and fold through the sugar. Put a tablespoon of the mixture into each peach.

5. Bake in the preheated oven for about 15 minutes, until the meringues in the peach halves are a light golden color. Serve immediately.

Crunchy cookies

After making this recipe, you can try kneading other ingredients into the dough. Instead of corn-flakes, try adding a handful of chopped nuts, raisins or chocolate drops. This recipe makes about 16 cookies. Preheat the oven to 350° F.

Ingredients
100 g all-purpose flour
50 g butter or margarine
50 g soft brown sugar
3 tablespoons milk
2 handfuls cornflakes

1. Sift the flour into a large mixing bowl. Using a small, sharp knife, cut the butter into small pieces. Drop them into the flour.

2. Work in (see p. 18) the butter and the flour.

6. Crumble the cornflakes over the dough. Knead the dough well by pressing it gently with your fingertips.

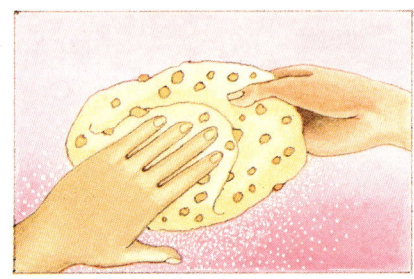

7. Turn the dough around, and fold the outside edges into the center as you knead. Knead until all the cornflakes are worked in.

8. Break off small pieces, each about the size of a walnut, from the dough. Roll each piece into a ball.

Chocolate pinwheels

To make this recipe, first follow steps 1–7 of the Crunchy cookies recipe and then start this one. These pinwheel cookies are ideal to serve at a party. Preheat the oven to 350° F.

Ingredients
100 g all-purpose flour
50 g butter or margarine
50 g soft brown sugar
3 tablespoons milk
2 handfuls cornflakes
25 g baking chocolate

1. Resting your fingertips lightly on a floured rolling pin, gently roll out the dough into an oblong shape about 20 cm x 15 cm. Use your hands to straighten the edges.

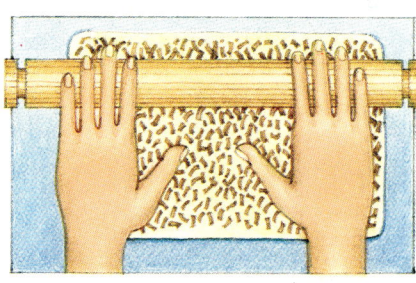

2. Using a coarse grater, grate the chocolate and sprinkle it over the dough. Use the rolling pin to press the chocolate gently into the dough.

3. Add the sugar to the mixture and quickly work it in.

4. Add the milk and use a spatula to mix everything together into a dough.

5. Sprinkle a little flour over your work surface. Put the dough onto it and use your hands to flatten the dough.

9. Place the balls of dough slightly apart on a cookie sheet. Use a fork to flatten them gently into cookies.

10. Bake in the preheated oven for about 20 minutes, until the cookies are a light golden brown. Carefully remove the cookie sheet from the oven.

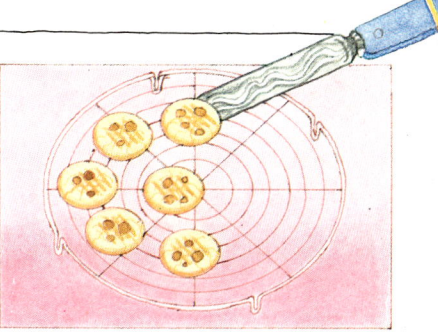

11. Leave the cookies on the cookie sheet for about 10 minutes to cool. Using a spatula, carefully put them onto a wire rack to finish cooling.

3. Starting with the long side that is nearest to you, roll up the dough into a sausage shape.

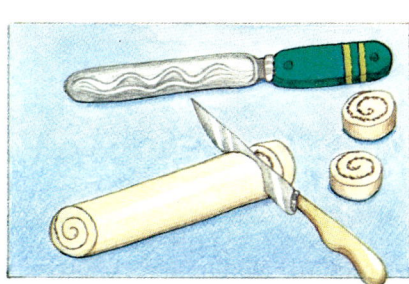

4. Using a large, sharp knife, cut the dough "sausage" into slices 1 cm thick.

5. Put the slices onto a cookie sheet and follow steps 10 and 11 of the Crunchy cookie recipe.